AF471624

IS A PREDATOR

ARE YOU A *Stressaholic*

stacey BLAKE

Edited by Mike Valentino

Cover design by Mannish

Publisher: Lightwalk Publishing, L.L.C.

paperback ISBN-13 978-1-942692-15-7
ebook ISBN-13 978-1-942692-14-0

Library of Congress Cataloging-In-Publication Data
Library of Congress Control Number: 2015909340

Printed in the U.S.A.

For You, Mom

I miss you every day

Mathew 11:28 (NIV)

"Come to me all you who are weary and burdened,
and I will give you rest."

Contents

Preface

In writing "Stress is a Predator: Are You a Stressaholic" my goal is to increase awareness of this condition…as many people suffer from it without even realizing they are afflicted (or how it happened). More importantly, I hope to plant the seeds necessary to initiate a commitment amongst professional researchers, therapists, psychologists, doctors and administrators of addiction centers, that there exists a real need for recovery programs specifically designed for "stressaholics".

The stressaholic needs a recovery program which differs from that offered for alcoholics, drug or food addicts. The key reason is that stressaholics are not inflicting injury upon themselves by way of ingesting harmful substances. They are being injured because they have unwittingly set into motion an internal chemical release (which resides within all of us) called the "fight or flight" response. Chronic overwork, the enormous pressures surrounding financial issues, intense professional duties and responsibilities, as well the emotional anxieties and worries about remaining competitive in business or in a career field (all) compounds within the mind and body. Overtime the cumulative effect of these factors will result in the body's "fight or flight" response turning on and never turning itself back off.

The consequence is a dangerous ***cocktail brew*** which circulates inside the individual and after a long period of time this will have a destructive effect upon their DNA, affecting overall health, emotions and spirit. In time physiological changes will affect their immune system. In advanced stages, many stressaholic's personalities begin to change. Someone who once possessed a very patient, kind and jovial personality might begin to display violent outbursts, aggressive behavior and abusive speech, issuing unrelenting demands upon others. Left untreated, a whole host of diseases can emerge.

I believe if caught early, before a serious illness happens, most stressaholics can reverse and recover from the debilitating effects of their chemical imbalance. If the stressaholic accepts and allows an understanding of what has happened to them to occur and how this reality came to be, they will be aided immensely in their able to participate in medicinal therapies which will turn their body's adrenaline/cortisol valve off. Once the 'fight or flight' response is under control, with proper rest, inner reflection, high-quality nutrition and rejuvenating therapy, a sustained healing of the mind, body and spirit will happen.

Everyone knows someone who is or has been a workaholic. In fact, today there are a few recovery programs designed specifically for "workaholics". There is though a very important differential between the workaholic and the stressaholic. A workaholic is typically defined as someone who works long hours because they are unable to set proper boundaries for themselves. It is a compulsive behavior rooted in an individual's personal preference. A workaholic may be physically healthy and happy but be disappointing family and friends by their addiction to hard work. The workaholic may actually be having a grand time of it without experiencing any negative health affliction at all. Or it may progress into something dangerous as it did for me; whereby the person becomes a stressaholic.

The stressaholic (is a workaholic) in that they possess all of the same compulsive behaviors with the big exception being they have set into motion a release of dangerously high levels of hormones referred as the"fight or flight" response. The mechanism to turn on this stress response generally happens when several chronic factors exist: i.e. a workaholic begins to suffer odd or pervasive fearful thoughts, when they begin to have intense anxieties, and when they can no longer relax and enjoy any quality personal private time they will eventually trigger this internal stress response to turn on....and remain on.

A proper treatment program for stressaholics should begin with a medical evaluation. Once their overall health is assessed an individual recovery regime can be prescribed. Depending on the level of one's physical/mental exhaustion, the presence of any disease, recovery programs may vary. However, once healing begins, it is absolutely essential that the stressaholic allow themselves to get adequate deep rest. This is the most important component for long term recovery. When recovered, the stressaholic must learn new stress management techniques to help them cope with the challenges of life and business without re-provoking the fight or flight response. It is complicated in many ways, but then again it is not. It is an addiction which needs to be properly addressed.

Introduction to the Stressaholic

Stress…how it affects the body and brain is a complicated subject. Symptoms, the how and when good stress turns into bad stress varies from person to person. It is a truth that good stress can be of great value in times of extraordinary difficulty. The "fight or flight" response exists within each of us for very good reasons.

The purpose of recounting about having been a stressaholic is to aid in the understanding of a subject hard to grasp…if not ever experienced. It is difficult even for those who find themselves to be stressaholics to understand exactly how it is they got there. It is not at all easy to articulate in exact terms the "when" and "how" someone transitions from being a healthy workaholic into an unhealthy stressaholic. It may be that specific blood tests will provide many of these answers but until this is commonplace the "stressaholic" today needs help, compassionate understanding and recovery.

Having been both a workaholic and a stressaholic, I believe the root of the transition lies in a chemically based ratio of too much work while chronic (subconscious) fear is present. Whether it can be measured in hours, days, weeks, months or years I cannot say, but at some point when sustained over a long period of time, the body's internal "fight or flight" switch turns on and when turned on it does not easily turn itself back off. Unlike a normal healthy person who's fight or flight response turns off when no longer needed, this is not the case for the stressaholic. It is a dangerous condition.

We live in a world where the majority of people grow up with preconceived judgements passed onto them by their parents and grandparents. If someone cannot relate or understand something they tend to dismiss or devalue it without a second thought. This is the way of human nature and it has been such for thousands of years. As long as outer appearances seem normal and things appear to be in "good order" then nothing "bad" is really going on.

I lived for years without anyone really understanding what was happening to me. I looked fine, I ran a good company and as far as outsiders could see, I was a success. Achieving such appearances took effort as I had to conceal, deflect and hide the truth of what was actually happening inside me. While I deeply loved the work and food products our company was making, my life was for years, one of quiet desperation.

Early in my adult life when I tried to speak on the enormous difficulties building a new food company from scratch was like–the response I got from loved ones was often one of sheer panic. I was advised to immediately stop what I was doing, shut the company down and take an easier, less demanding job. The reality is that when you are producing millions of dollars a year in sales, are hundreds of thousands of dollars in debt, you have 50+ employees, investors and retail customers all over the country this decision is unthinkable.

So, I stopped asking for help

As I describe in my first book, "A Soft Landing", after nearly committing suicide I was led to prayer. It was miraculous in so many ways. I was lifted up, I felt redeemed and I thrived. I secured incredible inner strength and I found ways to suspend fear, temporarily conquer difficulties and overcome.

And over the years I built a great company.

But I also became trapped. In my later years when opportunities to sell the company were presented, I found myself unable to accept. After becoming ill with leukemia and losing everything, I understand today (five years later) that I had in truth become "addicted" to my stress. I did not understand that the 'trigger' for my addiction was my having awakened the "fight or flight" response inside my body which in time strangled me.

I became a stressaholic

While many wonderful self-help books are on the market today offering proven techniques on how to de-stress, the fact is I had become something much more than a tension-filled entrepreneur. Once I was fully recovered from my leukemia and the loss of my business I realized the majority of books on stress management do not adequately address what exactly happens when a person becomes a stressaholic.

A physiological change occurs.

Many of us were taught while growing up to view "stress" as a nuisance issue of no real concern. Our parents and grandparents often believed that stress should simply be ignored–"Pretend that nothing bad is actually happening and (it) the symptoms will almost magically disappear." Admitting you were feeling "stressed" was akin to confessing a serious weakness, maybe as an attempt to perform less chores or work, like a child who claims they do not feel well to get out of going to school.

Such admissions are shunned

You will almost never hear a senior executive, doctor, lawyer or any other highly paid professional admitting openly that they are feeling "stressed". Nor will they admit to anyone that they may be waking in the middle of the night drenched in cold sweat or that sometimes during the day they might have to fight off a sudden impulsive feeling (that they want to scream at the top of their lungs) nor despite how incredible their outer lives appear, they cannot escape the constant feeling of being hunted or that they are suffocating.

A stressaholic is an individual caught in the grip of extraordinary stress and just like someone who is addicted to alcohol or drugs they are hunted daily by their addiction. For many stressaholics, attending a stress management seminar or reading one of the many books available on stress-relieving techniques is like handing an alcoholic a book on sobriety and telling them that after a good read they should be all set.

Where to begin?

The best place to comprehend how stress becomes like a predator is to understand that there is a progression. Stressaholics develop a type of (dis-ease) "disease" just as with any other addiction. To offer perspective on this I will share certain details about my own lifelong struggle with this plight, how it led (I believe) to my cancer, the failure and loss of all I worked my adult years for and how it is I live today in complete recovery.

I believe there is good news coming for stressaholics. There is significant new understanding in the medical and research fields on how chronic debilitating stress leads to major health problems–possibly even death. And there is growing awareness on how to combat such.

I hope that in sharing my story… *you who may be a stressaholic*, or if you love someone who you believe has become a stressaholic… will accept that seeking proper medical and/or therapeutic help is crucial.

Do not wait until it is too late.

Stressaholics should not need to get catastrophically ill, leave their business or company, they do not need to remain in the shadows, nor should they ever be treated like they are in need of psychological therapy.

Stressaholics are not mentally ill.

What this dis-ease needs is to be understood.

As with all addictions, the origins of becoming a stressaholic are often very subtle. There was a time when I could never have imagined writing the book you are reading today. But here I am and here we go…

Listen to Your Body

(*Excerpt from A Soft Landing*)
by: Stacey Blake

My story is one of many personal successes and challenges, but one very important piece of advice that I have for everyone is to listen to your body's silent signals that it will give you when something inside....is going wrong. The body is an amazing marvelous machine in many respects and it will try in odd ways to alert and warn you when "something" is going wrong deep inside.

Around the summer of 2008 I began to suffer episodes of paranoia that seemed at the time to come out of nowhere, plaguing me with intense feelings of fear that an imminent crisis of some kind was about to occur. It manifested for me in several ways. I had an Armageddon sense of doom that there would be a major weather disaster in our area, and to prepare to that I began to buy loads of dry goods, forcing my husband Tom to build for me extra shelves for all the canned goods and dried foods I was buying. On a beautiful day by the pool in the summers of 2007 and 2008 I would suddenly be affected by intense feelings of fear that an attack on the house by some dark "something" was about to happen and (quite honestly) I was forced several times to seek refuge inside my bedroom closet, where I would hide for hours. Imagine how I saw myself inside my closet while hiding. Here I was a successful businesswoman, whose company had for over twenty-five years grossed upwards of $100 million in sales, confidence inside me abounding – here I was hiding in fear of some unknown bogeyman – in my bedroom closet on a beautiful sunny summer day.

Today, I have come to believe that these impulsive feelings of fear were my body's attempt to warn me that "something on the inside of me" was going wrong. That illness was taking hold of me and I was becoming sick. Had I tuned into that more accurately I probably could have caught my leukemia at a much earlier stage.

For anyone who has suffered unexpected and bizarre fears, without any real basis in reality – please consider asking your doctor to do a complete physical exam with blood work.

Chapter One

How I became a Stressaholic

When I was in high school I was popular, athletic and an overall decent kid. I never partied, drank, experimented with drugs or hung out in cliques. I was a mentor to several young kids who lived in the 'projects'. For three years I was the captain of our school color guard and I was involved in many after school activities. This experience of having had a lot of respect from teachers and other students played a huge role in my personality and my sense of identity. It contributed to the super human expectations I placed upon myself and the inner desire and drive I developed: that I would absolutely succeed in everything I would come to do in life.

When I was 18 I left home to travel and work in Europe for one year. It was an amazing experience which grounded me in the absolute conviction that "someday" I would have my own money, be independent and live as I pleased. **Freedom** was my ultimate goal. I wanted more than anything to be free on the worries about money that consumed my family while I was growing up.

And I was willing to work as hard as I had to – to secure such.

After traveling Europe for one year I began college. I paid for my education on my own by working full-time at night as a bartender. I made great money and I was a solid student, but I had leaped into the cycle of chronic overwork at the tender age of 21.

My life routine solidified quickly. Wake 7:00 am. Drive to school 30 minutes away, classes from 10:00 am to 2:00 pm. Drive 30 minutes back home. Study, shower, and arrive at the restaurant by 4:30 pm. Work until 10:00 pm. Close down the bar, arrive home approx. 11 – 11:30 pm.

Weekends are supposed to be for fun and relaxation. But for me it meant working a double on Saturday and Sunday. I typically had two nights off work each week, which I used for studying. Summertime was not about vacation and lazy days at the beach. For me there were internships. It was a non-stop schedule and for the most part I thrived. It was at this stage in my early adult life that I began actualizing an inner belief, which first took root in high school that not only was I invincible, but that it was "expected of me" by others to be super human.

This false impression of myself was deeply imprinted within me. And it fueled every single decision I made. By age 24, a man I knew very well would become my business partner. By age 26; I was an entrepreneur.

Starting a new business is time consuming. Our business was in the food industry and the hours were excruciatingly long. But I was young, energetic and full of enthusiasm for what I knew we were trying to build. I never gave the long hours a second thought. We worked seven days a week, 14 hour days, every week, month and year for seven straight years.

By my 30th birthday I was an emotional wreck. I was an insomniac, I had suicidal thoughts and clearly I was under way too much stress. However, I loved the work we were doing and I strongly believed that what I was doing was exactly what was expected of me. Combined with the love I had for our food products, I simply ignored the slowly developing warning signs of how my schedule was overwhelming me.

I prayed every day for the strength to keep going and for the most part this worked wonderfully. So wonderfully, that I was able to keep up this ridiculous overwork schedule for far too many years.

Essentially, what began was a daily adrenaline response to my grueling work schedule. After several years, this adrenaline response never shut down. Cortisol and adrenaline flooded my body day in and day out. The "fight or flight response", a lifesaving systemic response our body produces, intended for sudden emergencies…for me this became a constant. Without this adrenaline and other internal hormones, I could not perform at the levels my duties and responsibilities demanded. Unwittingly, I had become addicted to my body's production of these hormones which I provoked the release of every day.

And I never suspected it for a minute.

Chapter Two

And so begin the steps to the end of my life as I had known it

By my early 30s my business was finally on its own two feet. Cash flow was positive, the company's bank account was sufficient and I was drawing a healthy paycheck. I was traveling two weeks a month to visit customer accounts and for the most part I was feeling quite successful. I never considered the toll working 80 hours each week was having on my health.

I allowed myself no time off. I was unable to relax in the true sense of the word. It never occurred to me that I was being overwhelmed in subtle ways I consciously never fully recognized.

When I tried to go for walks around the beautiful neighborhood I lived in, I could not do so for more than five minutes before intense feelings of "guilt" would engulf me that I should be back at the office on the phone, working and making things happen.

The truth is I mentally never really stopped working, even at 2:00 am when I got up to use the bathroom or to get a drink of water. When I had the opportunity to stay at a lovely resort during a business trip, I did not allow myself to enjoy the company of people I met, go out for a relaxing dinner or enjoy light conversation by the pool. At best, I was able to maybe enjoy a movie. Constant worry and mental activity about business matters from that day, the past week, the last month, future projects, company customers, its employees, and my business partners...all of it preyed upon on me every second of every day.

Internally, there was no "off" switch. I mentally was "working" while I ate breakfast, showered, was having lunch, preparing dinner and even while I was asleep. I dreamt about the business at night and this transitioned into incredible nightmares about floods, tornados, storms and dreams of being paralyzed or walking in mud or quicksand.

I was always mentally planning, re-planning, re-designing, re-discussing, and revisiting every single minute of every hour and every day I had experienced even during the times I was attempting to rest or visit family. I role-played meetings, negotiations, partner conversations over and over and over until I felt I had perfected any mistake I may have made or could possibly make in the future.

I worked 24/7 and eventually the positive energy that such mental activity (or "good" stress) would afford me, transitioned into something intensely dark and dangerous.

I could NOT slow down!

I actually did try to relax, but it was to no avail. An immediate surge of adrenaline would kick-in and I would re-cycle inside my mind again every single thought I had just processed earlier. This endless mental whiplash provoked actions and re-actions by me, which prompted more "hyper-activity" within the business that I then needed to, manage. The cycle of activity, reactionary activity and collapses voraciously fed on itself. After years of this mental rollercoaster I would need entire weekends to recover only to be recharged with adrenaline first thing Monday morning. I would internally provoke (unwittingly) a massive hormonal release to happen by way of my hyper-management style coupled with my obsessive need to be involved in all the details of <u>everything</u> that was happening inside the company.

Now, from a business point of view I was a dynamo. I produced outstanding results. However, I was drowning and dying internally as a person. I was not in any sense a healthy, wealthy or "free" business person. I was living inside a trap.

I had become a stressaholic

I was in deep trouble. I was utilizing prayer and spiritual practices such as meditation to try and keep up this inhuman pace and for many years, this worked. I would release some of the tension and stress. Yet for the most part I was offering only temporary relief for myself. After more than twenty years of chronic stress, my body began to breakdown.

I realize now that my body was desperately trying to alert me. It began to send warning signs that (dis-ease) was occurring. Dis-ease: meaning that my body was no longer at ease in any normal way. And while I believed I was doing good things for myself by way of naturopathic healing therapies, these therapies merely provided momentary relief from stress, and did nothing to eradicate what had become an internal ongoing "addiction" to adrenaline and all of the other associated hormones I was producing daily. I was working extreme hours because I literally ***could not work less***, the same way an alcoholic ***cannot drink less***–when their addiction wants to be fed.

And I did all of this to myself.

I do not have anyone else to blame or to shift responsibility onto. I had systematically over time become a stressaholic because I did not have the common sense to recognize I was working a ridiculously demanding schedule. I had become dependent on the internal production of dangerously high levels of adrenaline every moment of every day in order just to stand upright.

I was driving myself into the ground physically and mentally. Then, after ignoring all of the warning signs for two decades, my health broke down in a catastrophic way. I was diagnosed with CML Leukemia in July 2009. My particular CML was especially aggressive. I was given six months to live unless a successful stem cell donor transplant could be performed. Luckily, one of my brothers was a perfect match and in December 2009 I underwent a stem cell transplant. It took over four years for my body to recover.

To this day my immune system is not at normal levels but it is stronger than it was not too long ago.

I experienced complete devastation.

I describe in my book "A Soft Landing" what happened to me and I speak of how grateful I was that my faith in God helped me remain calm throughout my entire journey. However, I lost all that I had worked for as a result of my cancer and inability to return to my prior role as a CEO. Eventually, all that I had achieved and accomplished as a successful entrepreneur quietly passed away.

However, while it is true that I lost a great deal as a result of my leukemia, I found a far greater gift. I found myself. I discovered who I really am as a person, a soul, a human being freed from the debilitating effects of having become a stressaholic. I realize today how clouded my judgement had become about my personal priorities; enjoying life's simple pleasures and what truly is important in life.

I live today with the fervent hope that I can help others avoid such a life-altering consequence. It simply does not need to come to this for anyone.

Chapter Three

Understanding Stress

Stress affects everyone. It's a normal component of human life. In small doses, stress can even be beneficial. It can help motivate and inspire. It aids in the creative process, and it can assist you greatly when in distress or faced with grave danger. As a natural response to stress, your body becomes stronger and quicker to deal with difficult situations. This was particularly useful for our ancestors who dealt with threats from predators and the elements of nature. Vestiges may be seen in modern day activities such as "conquering" a particularly stressful workout at the gym, in competitive sports and within the military.

Stress (good stress) can help you feel exhilarated.

However, for some of us stress becomes a weapon that we turn against ourselves. High-achievers in business, entrepreneurs, professional athletes, and emotionally sensitive people who are very often care-givers, nurses, doctors and other medical professionals are especially vulnerable.

Don't be fooled into thinking that becoming a stressaholic is limited to any one type of profession or specific personality. Quite often people become stressaholics because they have been conditioned to accept chronic stress for a very long period of time (years) and over time the effects of the stress hormones and their constant release becomes devastating no matter who you are.

Given enough time, chronic stress affects every bodily system. Researchers estimate that 75-90 percent of all visits to primary care physicians are for complaints and conditions related in some way to stress. That's an amazing statistic! Just consider for a moment the staggering implications of it. Moreover, chronic stress plays a role in exacerbating a variety of other disorders and illnesses, such as cancer, diabetes, cardiac issues, and auto-immune diseases making it very hard for a person to heal or recover.

Who is the Stressaholic?

A stressaholic isn't always your typical type "A" personality who is hyper focused on output and optimum performance. Just because someone is mentally intense and razor sharp does not mean that they are a stressaholic. More accurately, a stressaholic is someone who through systemic and constant stress has **'turned-on'** their inner body's "fight or flight" response, releasing a constant flow of cortisol, adrenaline and other hormones into their body; and by way of constant daily stress, this natural (life-saving) inner body nervous system response

Never turns itself back off!

Flooded daily by these powerful bodily chemicals, the individual becomes dependent, "addicted" to the inner production of these natural life-saving hormones and chemicals in order to manage and keep up what is probably an inhumane schedule and set of demands.

When money and the financial needs of others are involved, it is a trap from which there is no easy escape.

Stressaholics live for the most part ruined lives. Of course, you will probably never know that. Most stressaholics appear successful, wealthy, privileged and free. (remember my personal goal of being "free"). In reality, nothing could be further from the truth. Stressaholics are not successful or wealthy in the ways that deeply matter. They are far from privileged and they most definitely are not free. Stressaholics are trapped inside a jail cell they personally built and then locked it with their own hands.

Just because someone may have the financial means to travel anywhere in the world, purchase anything they may desire and because they appear to have personal freedom does not mean they are "wealthy" or "free". If they are a stressaholic their inner soul, mind and body are being ravaged. They are being subjected daily to the destructive effects of the "fight or flight" response they have triggered and which is now preying upon them.

Worse yet, they have no idea what is going on or how they have contributed to it.

Night sweats, heart palpitations, interrupting others, loud speech, impatience with everything and everyone, constant demands to multi-task, use of profanity, headaches, body aches, stomach upset, bruising, inflammation in joints, insomnia, nightmares, trouble concentrating, and irritability are just a few of the initial warning signs that chronic overwork and stress is beginning to take a terrible toll. These are only a handful of serious physiological indicators that something very dangerous is beginning to happen within the body.

In and of themselves, of course, a small combination of any of these symptoms does not mean that a particular individual is now a stressaholic.

At least not yet

These early warning signs can be likened to the person who drinks heavily on weekends, but does not drink at all during the week. Or the individual who may have two to four drinks every night, but is not ***yet*** an alcoholic.

Everything is relative and this is especially true in the case of stressaholics.

It is a question of degree.

So when does an individual ***transcend*** chronic overwork and become a genuine stressaholic?

It is a quite an insidious happening.

Chapter Four

How Chronic Stress Leads to Other Diseases

Today the medical facts are indisputable that chronic stress is debilitating and left unresolved will eventually lead to devastating illness.

In my own case, during my years as a senior executive I became immune to the alarming symptoms that my body was sending me. I dismissed it all as being only *a little too much work.* I resigned myself to the belief that I was merely tired–as any hard working executive would be. But then, after 2008 my health fell into severe decline. And my body tried very hard to alert me that something was deeply wrong. (re: *Listen to Your Body-A Soft Landing*)

I had become such a micro-manager and this left no room within me for concern about what I was experiencing. Unexplained bruising would appear suddenly all over my body, I had terrible night sweats, frequent and reoccurring nightmares, sudden feelings of panic and paranoia, blurred eyesight, slurred speech, I would lose concentration during the day, I would become easily agitated and I suffered a constant bone weary exhaustion almost impossible to describe. I was suffocating.

At some point during 2008-2009 my leukemia birthed. Because I had become so good at dismissing all of my symptoms, I got sicker and sicker and I did not realize soon enough that I was in fact critically ill.

For the majority of people whom are not yet stressaholics, but believe and feel they are deeply affected by the negative effects of chronic stress, I offer here a brief list of some of the early warning signs you should not ignore.

Any combination of the following must be taken very seriously:

1. Disturbed sexual performance. While sex is a way of relieving stress, for those who are at the early stages of becoming stressaholic, sexual performance can become impaired. Disinterest due to loss of libido, premature ejaculation, erectile dysfunction and difficulty reaching orgasm are some of the issues. On the other hand, severe long term stress can provoke an insatiable sexual appetite to emerge which becomes itself an addiction.

2. Muscle and joint pain. When under severe stress, muscles will often contract and become tense. This in turn affects your nerves, blood vessels, skin, bones and organs. As stress progresses and becomes chronic it can result in a variety of other problems such as spasms, cramping, jaw pain, body tremors and loss of balance as well grinding of the teeth while sleeping. Muscle tension from excessive stress can lead to chronic migraines, chest and back pain, memory loss and a weakened ability to concentrate.

3. Chronic stress will affect the heart eventually. It can lead to coronary heart disease, sudden cardiac death and strokes. It can increase your blood pressure, constrict your blood vessels, raise cholesterol, trigger arrhythmias, and cause serious blood clots.

4. Gastrointestinal issues can develop. Chronic stress can affect the secretion of acid in the stomach and lead to constipation, diarrhea, gas, bloating and to sudden weight loss or weight gain. Especially provoked when there is a lot of business travel.

5. Trouble sleeping. Erratic sleep, insomnia, nightmares.

6. Apathy. Sudden feelings of worthlessness or insecurity. Loss of interest in things you used to love, family, work, sports and anything which used to be a source of great enjoyment.

7. Onset of alcohol abuse and/or drugs in order to cope.

8. Intense fatigue. Exhaustion.

9. Feelings of sudden panic or paranoia.

Chronic stress will eventually affect the body's immune system, too. In fact, researchers have a name for the study of this phenomenon- "psychoneuroimmunology". Psychoneuroimmunology is the study of how chronic stress compromises the immune system, causing mood swings, erratic emotional states and it studies how stress directly disturbs the body's hormonal balance in (cortisol, adrenaline) leading to a dangerous change in the body's nervous system and immune system.

Researchers have shown that chronic debilitating stress will play a role in exacerbating a variety of immune system disorders such as HIV, AIDS, and herpes. Moreover, researchers know today that chronic stress can provoke the development of cancer, rheumatoid arthritis, viral infections, as well as several auto-immune diseases.

So, with all of this new scientific information and medical confirmation on the damaging effects of chronic stress, why do so many people continue to fall into negative behavior patterns leading to debilitating stress? And in extreme circumstances leading them into becoming stressaholics?

As someone who has been a stressaholic, let me try to explain.

Career, business needs, and money, (the so-called pursuit of the American dream) require inordinate amounts of time and attention focused on work. Networking, which includes professional associations and all the activities related to it, at the end of the day leaves no time for calmness and activities which are relaxing.

The brain becomes super-charged all the time.

Baby Boomers were raised and strongly encouraged to be high-achievers. Status, educational degrees, income, obtaining a beautiful home, owning multiple cars, the display of outward signs of wealth in general is what most

Baby Boomers were taught to use as the measuring stick for their personal achievement and success.

The onset of instant communication via cell phones, iPad, tweeting, Facebook, Google and social media in general has added a turbo-like fuel to an already overly stressed culture. And when money is the focus and goal…the game of life becomes especially intense, mentally, emotionally and physically.

Baby Boomers have learned to prioritize by placing their personal needs for quiet time and self-reflection on the back burner. Engrained in one's mindset over many years, this state of being becomes almost impossible to change and correct.

Chronic work and stress pervasively interferes and disturbs one's ability to disengage, turn inward and seek inner nourishment away from the noise of daily life.

Stressaholics typically have enormous professional and personal responsibilities.

Letting go is unthinkable.

As with me, I neglected and ignored all the warning signs in favor of: another sale, a larger new customer and weeklong trips to monitor business projects, midnight emails and constant oversight of daily administrative operations.

I was very reluctant to engage in any professional socialized activities which could have provided some stress release and recreation. As a CEO I viewed that within such professional encounters…might lay a significant vulnerability. Industry collusion, sabotage, intrigue of all kinds is a fact of life here in America. And most if not all senior executives and CEO's lose sleep worried about how such networking activities can potentially affect their company's security and future. It is believed networking is always a positive business activity. But, for many executives there is an undercurrent of stress, worry and fear as to who can and cannot be trusted. And while an executive will very often participate in the many golf and ski outings, meetings and retreats, the interaction is often light and superficial. The consequence is that the stressaholic cannot tell someone else who *might understand* what is occurring to them or how it is they are suffering.

The other truth is that very often fellow members of professional organizations are 'fair weather' friends. When complex and difficult problems arise for an executive… peer friendships may suddenly become chilly, distant or abruptly disconnected. As well, the truth is that often the fellow members of any professional industry group–always "*know*" people…who "*know*" your competitors…and they "**know**" the companies who wish to defeat or copy the products and services you produce. So while it appears as though everyone who belongs to these associations all are very close friends – this often is an illusion!

Self-preservation dictates silence.

Silence for the stressaholic means that they are churning privately their deepest fears without a safe outlet. Over time, this will cause a stressaholic to feel extremely lonely, angry, betrayed and they will consequently lash out at those closest to them…most especially loved ones and loyal employees.

It is essential that researchers and therapists working to help conquer debilitating stress understand that the stressaholic who is most in need of help and recovery is often reserved and very quiet. While in social situations they will cautiously guard their deepest worries and concerns about their business issues in fear that any such admissions may be used against them in the future.

With the right kind of addiction recovery and understanding the stressaholic will gain important personal and professional perspective. Once they see clearly what they have unwittingly done to themselves and how it all came about – I believe they will surrender to the healing process and recover quickly.

Knowledge is a powerful healer. Think about someone you know who is deeply afraid to fly and so they do not fly. In many cases once this person understands the "how" and "why" an airplane remains up in the air… very often this knowledge releases their fear immediately.

Knowledge is the pathway forward for healing and long term recovery. Every stressaholic needs to learn what has been happening inside their bodies and the **power** they have to stop it.

Without this understanding and recovery, stressaholics run a very high risk of becoming devastatingly ill.

All true healing begins with the right understanding, the right perspective and the right mindset.

For myself, I did not have this knowledge in time to save me from becoming ill with leukemia and because of that I lost everything. However, in my loss, I discovered something. I discovered the person I always knew I was and could be. Once I was healed and free of my addiction to stress I learned that I am the happiest with less responsibility; less worry over money, and no striving at all for corporate success.

Today, I am a writer of both inspirational and children's books. I work a quiet schedule. I allow myself as much rest and sleep as I need. I take gentle walks. I do not ever feel rushed, pushed, and I never feel the need to do anything I do not wish to do.

And as a result my body has healed. While I am not and never will be a totally healthy person who never experienced leukemia and chemotherapy, radiation, and drugs, I am so grateful to still be alive and aware today as to what exactly happened to me and how it is I allowed such to happen. I had unwittingly, innocently and systematically become a stressaholic. I hope that in telling my personal story, you too who may be a stressaholic… can feel within yourself the longing to be free of all your silent suffering.

The deepest spiritual truth for me is my leukemia was a blessing. It made a part of my life which needed to end – end. And while I am very lucky to be alive, I live with the hope I can help others never be as blind as I was.

I realize that it is a truth, that if I had read my own story written in someone else's hand back in 2008/2009 I would have outright ignored it.

In my book, "Today Creates Tomorrow," I write about how personal choice is the basis for everyone's reality. What you do today affects your tomorrow. It is simple really.... and yet it is not so simple. We go through our days so distracted we become unconscious. Often the sub-conscious takes control. And the sub-conscious is where everyone's insecurities, childhood fears and fear-based beliefs reside.

This reality leaves every person vulnerable to the negative effects of stress. Throw in some alcohol and drugs in order to cope and you have a recipe for disaster.

I hope that if you have found your way to my book, and you recognize yourself in what I am describing, you will allow my voice to penetrate.

Specific help and recovery for Stressaholics remains to a high degree undeveloped. For me, I had to be completely flattened by my cancer. I was in bed for over one year, restricted within my home for almost two years and when I tried after year two to go back to work, I got severely ill all over again. What I thought was a sound professional commitment to working was in actuality stubbornness. An inability to 'get it', and a refusal to 'accept' what had been happening to me.

I did not yet understand what would now need to be my new reality. Eventually, after a great deal of suffering, I did get it. I understood the consequences of my cancer and my having become a stressaholic. It took a couple years for me to appreciate that I was so physically devastated by my cancer and my relapses that it meant I would never be able to go back to my career as a senior executive. Nor could I engage in any professional activity of responsibility in which severe "stress" would be provoked.

Just as with an alcoholic who cannot ever drink again – stress, excessive stress, could never happen to me again. If I allow it–a severe heart-attack or stroke could be the result. **Stress does kill**. I was very lucky.

At some point in everyone's life you come face-to-face with yourself whether you want to or not. Hopefully, when this happens for you or someone you love, the decision will be made to immediately implement a proper course correction.

I rely on my faith in God and my belief that this world is good to sustain me. I know deep in my heart and soul that I am never alone and that I do not need to prove anything to anyone, most especially myself.

I live today with a much different mission, purpose and perspective. One that I hope resonates with you, especially if you are facing significant decisions in order to transcend chronic stress and heal your mind and body.

Chapter Five

Why stress is so hard to defeat

Stress is a predator. It stalks you without you ever knowing it. It creeps up on you, it lurks in the background, it slips back, moves forward, hides and just when you think you are in the clear – it attacks.

You may go years without having any idea that stress is stalking you. Going about your hectic daily routine, you embrace projects and assignments with enthusiasm. For most people, this is perfectly okay. But there is a time when warning signs may begin to appear. You find yourself feeling fatigued for no real good reason. You are not sick; you have not caught flu or a cold, yet a nagging feeling of something not being just right keeps gnawing upon your psyche.

You ignore it and so it passes.

But then symptoms begin to ramp up. Your dreams at night become confusing and vivid. Reoccurring dreams may include visions of a flood, a fire, a tornado or a scene where a bridge is down and you cannot cross over to where you need to be. You wake with the back of your neck covered in cold sweat; your entire body may be drenched with perspiration. But you dismiss all of these warning signs. If you're a woman maybe you just assume it is the onset of menopause. Or if you're a man you simply pretend nothing is happening. Yet it's becoming increasingly difficult to keep deluding yourself. It may progress with you waking up in a state of panic. You may want to scream at the top of your lungs. Or quite possibly you have feelings of fear but you don't know exactly why. Nighttime disturbance is a very significant alarm bell that your body and your mind are under severe duress. Stress way too much stress is occurring.

But–you have that 6:00 wake-up call, a flight scheduled at 8:00 am taking you to a meeting at 1:00 pm; and giving any thought to these seemingly strange happenings is immediately stomped on and banished to the far corners of your mind where you've kept all such notions tucked away.

Who has time to worry about apparent nonsense?

You have too many responsibilities! So, you ignore these symptoms and afterwards many others.

Those of us whose nervous systems ultimately became compromised and whose bodies may now be overproducing the "fight or flight" response will sooner or later start experiencing a new combination of warning symptoms. Headaches, body aches, forgetfulness, sudden feelings of panic during the middle of the day, nervousness, fatigue and agitation, mood swings, sudden abusive outbursts to those around you, constant tapping of fingers, feet, swinging of a leg, staring off when you're being spoken to; you rudely interrupt others, jump up out your chair out of the blue, pacing or walking in circles, one drink too many at lunch or dinner, use of drugs to try and relax, etc. No doubt about it, there is an overall general destructive pattern happing inside your body; yet again, however, you ignore each and every symptom because for the most part, another topic or business issue is of course far more important than all of this inconsequential nonsense.

Sound familiar?

Two of the most serious warning signs that I can personally relate and attest to, pointing to a person that has *eclipsed chronic stress and is now a stressaholic*, are the sudden feelings of panic and paranoia.

You however may find yourself instigating arguments with employees, partners, family, and friends. Though you don't consciously realize it, there's a very goal-driven reason for this: like a spark plug, arguments can facilitate the ignition or inner charge of adrenaline and other hormones, lifting an exhausted person from feelings of near collapse, to a heightened state of super-charged energy. This powerful surge, which stressaholics crave, is directly related to the "fight or flight" response.

For myself, the way that I ignited this trigger switch was byway of my hyper intensive focus on every single detail of the business. Every day, upon awakening bone weary tired, I would make few phone calls that required a thorough reporting of production status, sales, financials, administrative controls, etc. I ran the company with verification, re-verification procedural process that was microscopic. After a few initial phone calls, coffee and a daily briefing at the office I was fully totally energized! It worked all the time, every day, like magic.

As the body becomes continuously run-down, the mind recognizes the “fix” that the hormonal chemicals of the fight or flight response provides. By unwittingly provoking terrible arguments or in my case intensified daily reporting and analysis the stressaholic is spinning up energy to feed off of. Not only does this activity indicate severe physical ‘dis-stress’ but in some cases emotional dis-stress as well.

Unconsciously endangering a happy home or a well-run company in order to feed an addiction of missing adrenaline means that destruction of everything and everyone that individual loves *may be just around the corner...*

For stressaholics, the constant need for adrenaline day after day, month after month and year after year, is inevitably leading to their demise. The stressaholic’s pathway to get their life and health under control will evaporate over time. Their body and mind will break. In advanced stages it simply will become a question of when and in what form it will take.

Chapter Six

The Nature of Stress

Webster's Dictionary defines stress as – "a state of mental or emotional strain or tension resulting from adverse or very demanding circumstances".

The American Institute of Stress states on its website – "Stress is not a useful term for scientists because it is such a highly subjective phenomenon that it defies definition". They go on to explain there is both "good stress" and "bad or tension related stress", which everyone experiences.

Neither of these definitions, however, properly defines stress from the point of view of a stressaholic. Webster's does not have a definition for a stressaholic. However, I predict someday soon they will.

A possible definition of a stressaholic might be–*an individual whose physical body is producing pathologic or extraordinary amounts of cortisol and adrenaline which can be measured via blood tests and examination of the patient's adrenals, lymphatic system, kidneys, blood pressure, internal ulcerations, or an onset of chronic heart or breathing difficulty. The onset of any number of other diseases can be directly correlated back to chronic debilitating daily stress.*

I believe one of the reasons why proper diagnosis and recognition of a "stressaholic", as a disease, (such as alcoholism) has not happened to date, is individuals who are suffering such either do not recognize what is happening to them or they do recognize, but are too embarrassed to acknowledge it…especially to others.

There is shame in labels

The person needing help may be concerned that being diagnosed in some specific way (such as a stresshollic) might connote that they are "out of control", possibly "reckless", "mentally ill" and maybe "untrustworthy". All of these labels are incorrect. The vast majority of individuals who are probably stressaholics are most likely extraordinarily competent professionals. They are producing fantastic results monetarily for their companies and for themselves. Yet they are deeply injured souls and will continue to get progressively ill if they do not receive proper treatment and undertake efforts to bring an immediate end to the ongoing "fight or flight" response that their bodies are triggering in an automatic and uncontrolled manner.

The other reason why I believe there has not yet been a proper classification for this dis-ease – is that unlike an alcoholic who puts the chemicals into their own body by their own hand, which is an observable act – stressaholics have an ongoing reactionary *internal* chemical response which is not observable. Therefore, to the outsider, nothing is actually happening. That is extremely deceptive! Something very serious and with dire consequences is indeed happening and it may be detectable through proper testing and diagnosis; however, the person affected must first submit to such evaluation.

As mentioned earlier, the onset of becoming a stressaholic is subtle and often innocent. However, the ongoing process and progress of the dis-ease evolves insidiously. It happens slowly and without real announcement, which is what makes chronic stress (combined with fear) such a deadly killer. Unlike a person who ingests too much alcohol, whereby they feel the effects and are drunk, the stressaholic is uplifted and empowered by the increased levels of adrenaline. Their minds are sharp, they are quick footed in their responses and they oftentimes feel invincible. And for a time, they are.

So the goal here is twofold. First, to increase awareness of the process and progress of what starts out always as "good stress" but over time converts internally into a triggering of unhealthy levels of the "fight or flight" response; causing addiction to these hormonal chemicals to occur. For those who are deeply affected and are now stressaholics, the second goal is to aid in their ability to find the right kind of medical and therapeutic help. Of course, depending on the individual and their circumstances allowing outsiders to help them may take enormous courage. As is often the case it becomes a question sometimes as to the degree of suffering an individual must experience before they will take firm action. This is the most difficult conundrum facing many stressaholics. Admitting soon enough "they" are heading down the wrong path…and that in time they the “workaholic” will become the “stressaholic” whose very life might become endangered.

Knowing and recognizing early enough that a few of the symptoms I speak about are a **warning sign** is what I hope to see achieved in telling my own story.

Full recovery is possible if caught early enough and reversed. Or the alternative as with what happened to me–the stressaholic may possibly lose everything maybe even; their own life.

I think here of Steve Jobs.

Steve Jobs was a true business visionary. However he was considered cruel, verbally abusive and demeaning to his loyal employees and it is known that he was incapable of slowing down his inner drive, his constant demands and his incredible schedule. Steve Jobs built an amazing company. But, he lost his life while still in his prime. And it is said by those who knew him that Steve Jobs understood near the end that he had a hand in his own health’s demise.

There are many other men like Steve Jobs, like Jeff Bezos, who clearly were or are stressaholics. Each built extraordinary products and companies and each is known to have been quite vicious, demanding, cruel and verbally abusive to those around them. Some of these men maybe worse than others, but each exhibited all of the signs (in my opinion) of a highly addicted stressholic.

Chapter Seven

The catastrophic component of fear

Observers of extraordinary visionary leaders like Steve Jobs will comment that such bad behavior is rooted in their insecurity. (i.e. Tony Schwartz – The bad behavior of Visionary Leaders (NY Times – June 26, 2015))

I have to disagree. What is misunderstood as insecurity is in fact "fear". Fear that churns deep inside every stressaholic. Fear of failure, fear of disappointing so many people who believe in your dreams, fear of not being effective, fear of not having competent execution, fear that others are conspiring against you, fear that your product or products will fail, fear that someone will copy or infringe upon your company, fear that you (yourself) are not doing everything fast enough, good enough and that in the end you will let others down and that you will be the reason your company fails. This fear energy churns inside most extraordinary visionaries like Steve Jobs, but it also exists within many senior executives, doctors, financial executives, entrepreneurs, some political leaders and even educators.

Insecurity has nothing whatsoever to do with what drives extraordinary leaders. This is an incorrect judgement made understandably by observers who have not *walked in the other person's shoes.* The size of Steve Jobs' company or

Elon Musk or even Jeff Bezos has nothing at all to do with the important deeper understanding and appreciation that (chronic fear) combined with (chronic overwork) is the deadly cocktail inside most stressaholics.

My personal and professional observation has been that insecure business people often cannot summon for long periods of time the courage and the energy to produce sustained outstanding results. The catalyst of energy necessary does not bloom. The "juice" needed just isn't there. Insecure people cannot sustain the inner will, the inner desire, to succeed through the adversities that strike every single new entrepreneur. Somehow and in some manner they will sabotage their own efforts.

To an outside observer what they believe they are seeing as insecurity is in fact fear. I can state with firsthand knowledge that the catalyst is fear; a lot of fear. Very often it is fear of failure. Oftentimes, it lies within the person's subconscious. Fear though is the turbo fuel which turns workaholics into stressaholics. Overtime, compounded chronic debilitating overwork, overthinking, and fearful worries and anxiety will lead some to commit perverse and abusive behavior, as noted by many who study extraordinary visionary leaders. It is their "disease", their stressaholic condition, which is the root cause for their abusive behavior. Fear is the trigger…..and it lurks silently underneath all the outer signs of significant wealth, entrepreneurial success, staggering confidence and visionary leadership.

For those individuals and business leaders who are suffering only 'modest' levels of daily stress and tension, there are many articles, books and speakers today that discuss the beneficial and successful methods proven to release built-up tension and stress. They offer and prescribed very sound techniques on how to prevent "good stress" from developing further.

There are many self-help practices which almost anyone can implement to aid in overcoming short-lived stress and tension i.e. prior to business meetings, presentations, confrontations, and difficult negotiations. Anyone facing a stress-filled event can be overwhelmed by their circumstances causing slight damage to their nervous system. If repetitive and sustained it, will lead to physical difficulties but at an early stage it is very controllable.

None of these self-help stress management tactics will work for the person who has become a full-fledged stressaholic. Stressaholics suffer an acute, automatic internal chemical release of cortisol and adrenaline each and every day. It is an entirely different kind of problem and degree of dis-ease. It is extreme and it requires specific recovery and remedy.

Chapter Eight

How to stop stress before it's too late

Coping with stress is not easy. While I knew for many years that something was just not right inside me, I could not find the inner-will or courage to change or stop the stress even though it was absolutely debilitating me.

The demands and responsibilities of leading the company I helped build, the inner fear I harbored that stopping or slowing down could mean the loss of millions, the loss of professional credibility for the company and its products, the erroneous belief that no other field of work would make me happy, that my life and identity would lose any meaning and that I could not "do" anything else, all disrupted and blocked my ability to think clearly and to understand what I had become.

For those workaholics who have not yet become stressaholics, there are a variety of ways to blunt stress and control its effects before it's too late.

Within this book's glossary are a handful of excellent resources, books and websites available for more in-depth reading on current research and new studies as to the harmful effects of stress on the body, methods and techniques to relieve stress, as well as a number of very reliable practices to aid in stress prevention.

The way forward and out of chronic stress
starts always with a mindset.

Reduce stress by taking care of yourself. Chronic stress will ultimately interfere with your ability to see yourself first as a person who must take care of you! More than likely your stress is a result of you taking care of family, a company, an employer, fellow employees, someone else.

The highest truth is that the stronger you are as an individual, the better able you are to do your job, take care of your home and to stay healthy. Chronic stress will rob you of resiliency, leading to you to feel fatigued, fearful and sick.

Taking care of **YOU** is the first major priority. As soon as you begin to feel overwhelmed and exhausted, take two steps back and re-evaluate what it is you are doing. Simple reprioritization will help tremendously. Begin to approach tasks one at a time. As you begin to make positive lifestyle choices for yourself you will immediately notice a reduction in stress within yourself.

The way I remain stress free today is aided immensely by the following:

1. Get Moving – exercise, gentle walks, yoga, Thai Chi, standing up at your desk or getting up off the couch and doing ten jumping jacks, stretching, doing knee bends and even just a brisk walk up and down the nearest stairs a few times can do wonders. The key

is to blunt tension, muscle pain and fatigue as soon as you recognize the signs.

2. Keep your blood sugar stable. Food choices are one of the greatest ways to prevent the onset of strcss and feelings of fatigue. There are many helpful books and websites to refer to.

3. Take a relaxing bath. Twenty minutes in warm water with soothing bath salts can yield incredible immediate results.

4. Drink Alcohol moderately and avoid all recreational drugs.

5. Get enough sleep. Consider adding naps into your day whenever you can. It is a fact that a 10-15 minute nap will refresh your body and your mind allowing you to be more productive, help you to recall facts and information faster and it will lift your mood.

6. Reach out to friends for support. Stressaholics often become introverts. When you feel the need to talk to someone, ask the person you trust the most for their time. Make it clear you need them to help you release tension and stress with personal time for (maybe) a long talk, a spa day, a walk, a trip to the movies and dinner, etc. Be totally upfront that you need help in their 'being' with you. A trusted friend will understand and take it from there.

7. Create a balanced schedule. Eliminate multi-tasking to the highest degree possible. It will help more than you can imagine!

8. Learn to say NO. I could write a book on this one step alone. The point is to realize that you must set priorities according to what you need to stay stress free and healthy. As soon as someone asks something of you and you feel that 'twinge' inside yourself; whereby you feel imposed upon – say NO. Say it lovingly, politely, kindly; but say NO. You will not believe how incredibly strong you will feel afterwards.

9. Don't overcommit on activities, entertainment or any other job responsibility. Know your limitations, respect them and set boundaries.

10. Be willing to compromise. The ability to compromise on problems, negotiations, issues within the home, your spouse, will aid you tremendously in living stress free.

11. Delegate, delegate, delegate. The ability to allow others to perform tasks for you is invaluable.

12. Become self-aware. Learn to recognize when your mood swings, know when you become fatigued, angry, confused and conflicted. Incorporate coping techniques that work for you quickly and you will gain control over all aspects of your emotions. You will no longer feel victimized or whiplashed.

13. Try to develop perspective on why challenges always exist. Using humor is a great way to dispel stress before it overwhelms you. Recognize that life is not always going to be easy, that people often will disagree and that you must avoid the emotional disturbance that anger creates. My book "Today Creates Tomorrow: How Destiny Lies in Your Hands," could be extremely helpful. A simple change in inner perspective could be the most healing and liberating act you could ever do.

There are numerous other ways to help you overcome and defeat stress. Some of the best ways are quite simple. Keep a neat work area. Do away with messy closets, shelves, and countertops. Remain silent when you feel unprepared to address an issue. Give praise to others who help and assist you. Flip your perspective when you do not agree on a matter at work or home. Take a moment to ask yourself why or how it is the other person sees the situation so differently than you do. You will be amazed at how often five minutes of quiet reflection will yield new ways of agreement you never thought possible. This is only achievable when you are in a calm state of self-control and not affected unduly by hormonal influences.

Chapter Nine

Personal Choices

Ultimately everything in life comes down to personal choices. We choose what type of person we will become by every decision we make. Life and what happens to us is guided by our own hands.

Why we draw negative experiences to ourselves has been an age old question for which the same answer applies. We choose to experience these things in order to grow. And we do most of it unconsciously.

Choosing to live free from stress needs to be learned. Just as entire generations have been taught not to smoke, drive while drunk or to text while driving, people need to be taught at a very young age how to live stress-free.

If begun early enough in a young person's life, the wonderful self-help techniques to release stress and tension could last a lifetime! The ability for anyone to be able to recognize the signs of uncontrolled stress within themselves early enough means that the negative effects of stress and the illness that follows can be blunted. I whole heartily hope and pray that many of the stress management techniques known are taught as early as high-school and most definitely by college.

Proper stress management education, self-help techniques and recovery methods are a must. My leukemia was like hitting a brick wall. I had to stop working. I could no longer work. And it took me years to fully accept this new reality for myself.

Today, I am no longer a stressaholic. I have been able to see all of what happened to me so clearly. However, as with any alcoholic, I cannot introduce stress in any form back into my life. I can immediately feel a change happen within my body whereby triggers occur and signals are sent. My eyes blur, my heart pounds, my speech sometimes will slur and in general, fatigue overwhelms me almost instantly. I can lose my balance walking and a sudden feeling of suffocation occurs.

I cannot tolerate any pressures such as deadlines, hurriedness, heated negotiations, etc. These types of triggers are intolerable and I do all that I can to avoid them being a part of my daily life.

The manifold benefits of my new lifestyle are glorious! Without stress, I live a peaceful, productive life as a writer. I sip my coffee each morning, I enjoy gentle walks, and I take enormous pleasure in my animals, cooking a meal, taking a long boat ride with my husband and reading.

I have accepted that my soul lives in a damaged body that cannot do the things it used to do…**but I am alive**! I am alive and I am free from much of what I used to believe was so important. And of course at the time a lot of it was important. But I did not do any of it in a healthy, balanced manner. While I accept that this was my path to spiritual learning and self-discovery, I hope with all my heart that with the proper information younger generations can be educated how to avoid, stop and spot the warning signs of debilitating stress.

Chapter Ten

Helping Yourself and Others to Live Stress-Free

There are dozens of incredibly good books, handbooks, lecturers and medical researchers talking about the proven ways to keep stress under control and how to use good stress as a tool.

I hope to encourage these extraordinary professionals to work together in the promotion and formation of organizations and recovery groups specifically designed for stressaholics. To help advocate and bring into the open a way for exhausted executives and distressed individuals to find effective recovery help without losing all that they have worked for their entire lives, most especially their health and mental well-being and their very lives.

Just as with binge drinking and abuse of alcohol and drugs; stress can progress when everything and everyone around you is stressed.

Stress begets Stress

Households that do not wish to encourage alcohol use typically do not display bottles of liquor as decoration. Banishing stress is no different.

Living stress-free within a home or office begins in simple ways. Here are some suggestions:

1. Lower your voice. Shouting is a huge trigger for stress. Once it begins it can turn the whole household upside down. This affects young children most negatively. It is my number one suggestion for all families and parents to understand. Stop shouting!

2. Speak without the use of force (unless absolutely necessary). This is a different issue than shouting. In the office, at home, issuing **orders** with ***force*** produces a vibration of threat. It provokes fear. Those nearby will feel this energy and in-turn process an immediate instinctual need to protect themselves. And for many, the stress response (fight or flight) kicks in. If this happens too often, daily or weekly, a cycle of chronic stress begins and it will continue unless deliberate conscious behavior changes are made.

3. Recognize the signs of stress progression in yourself and others. Pay attention to the early warning signs, i.e. insomnia, interrupting others, vulgar language, headaches, abusive speech, berating of others, pacing, irritability and forgetfulness are all indications that stress is present and taking a toll. Instead of placing blame, shame and issuing more demands, try to understand if there is a deeper systemic stress issue happening within the person you love or work with. As with someone who is at the early stages of using too much alcohol in order to cope, become aware of the signs of too much stress. Be gentle, loving, and

compassionate. Stress stopped early enough can be totally eliminated and turned into a good positive use of energy.

4. Compromise. Learn to compromise. Horrific stress will engulf you the more entrenched you become in disagreements. Anger, resentment, feelings of betrayal, attachment to outcomes–all can accumulate and fuel intense stress. It may require professional help but learn how to distance yourself emotionally and see the other person's point of view. This can transform your life entirely and allow you the ability to eclipse and better manage any difficult circumstance that may arrive during your life.

As someone who was a stressaholic it is essential for long-term recovery that you seek immediate help from a doctor or therapist that you trust, and that at all cost, you secure distance from your job, career or business if necessary.

For stressaholics you must accept that abstinence from stress is a must. You cannot recover with the self-help techniques that work for those who have mild tension and some stress, but have not triggered the hormonal changes which are happening now within you. This is the key differential you must allow, accept and surrender to. Your life may depend on it.

IF you have tried everything you can to bring balance and healing into your life, such as meditation, prayer, time-outs, exercise and maybe even attended a stress management seminar and you have read self-help books on how to release stress; but you are still under chronic dis-stress and suffering many physical symptoms….you must **completely** unplug. You must leave for a time whatever is the situation. Your job, your company, your marriage, whatever it is. You must take a long time-out. As someone who has been a stressaholic, I know that it takes months to heal. You simply will not secure healing while the triggers continue to exist within you.

I am well aware that at this time there may not be recovery centers or sanctuaries specifically for the stressaholic, but with the right understanding and medical diagnosis you may find that very soon there will be a way to facilitate the necessary time off you may need, without having to throw the baby out with the bathwater, such as what happened to me. My body made my decisions for me and in time, everything unraveled.

It is a universal truth that those with whom we choose to live and work affect our lives, our mind and our physical health in profound ways. *YOU must take control of your own future destiny and accept that living stress-free is always a personal choice.* ***No one else has the power to make that decision for you…except for that remarkable individual staring back at YOU in the mirror.***

Frequently Asked Questions

How can I be sure that I'm really a stressaholic and not just going through a stressful period in my life?

If you are experiencing sudden outbursts at those who work for you and at home, you have constant nightmares, sweating, or are experiencing sudden feelings of panic or paranoia; for certain you must see your doctor. A stressful period of time such as the death of a loved one, the loss of a job or a disappointing event does not cause you to become a stressaholic. For these times, stress-relieving techniques are very helpful. The presence of chronic fear (even if only subconscious) combined with chronic overwork (long hours week after week, month after month, year after year) sets the stage for an individual becoming a stressaholic. It is a question of degree. A person suffering from a migraine should not jump to the immediate conclusion that they may have a brain tumor.

What if I suspect that someone close to me is a stressaholic, what should I say to him/her?

There is not a simple answer. Depending on your relationship I would tread carefully. Typically, depending on the degree of suffering or problems they may be facing, if they are in a supercharged mental state due to adrenaline they will not "hear" you. If they are starting to become paranoid and are in advanced stages of becoming a stressaholic they may very easily misunderstand your intentions. This is where the help of a professional skilled in stress management techniques will be very helpful. The sooner an afflicted person is helped the better. The more advanced the disease the harder it is for the individual to recognize it. Just think again on the alcoholic. With a stressaholic, the person you care about is being afflicted by powerful bodily chemicals. They are momentarily blinded by the hormones their body is producing. At a minimum get them to their primary doctor for a physical exam and blood work. It is one step at a time. One possible aid could be to videotape the person when they are having a symptomatic response – like shouting, screaming at employees, pacing, etc. Do it quietly. Review afterwards. Ask for professional help. I have known of situations whereby those who view their tantrums by videotape can be helped tremendously–if it was presented to them without any sense of judgement. Remember, their condition progressed slowly and often innocently. Do everything with love, especially if you know the person harbors subconscious fear of failure. Their self-preservation instinct will be well exercised. At all times take things slow until they are able to "see" what has occurred to them.

Does the medical profession recognize all of this as a legitimate disorder, and if so what treatments do they suggest?

I would say that they are beginning to. There is a lot of new research and studies being written on how chronic stress affects health. Even the person who is not yet a stressaholic but does have high anxiety and cannot slow down their minds needs to take seriously whatever help is available. For the true stressaholic — whereby the element of fear is combined with too much work — this specific situation requires more understanding as a differential. That will come in time when there have been successful interventions for those stressaholics who have allowed themselves to be helped.

The adrenal glands may help provide clues. Adrenal exhaustion is one sign that an individual has been producing too much cortisol, etc. This will contribute to chronic fatigue and the subconscious need to provoke a fix. This is the insidious nature of the stressaholic condition.

In your own case, was there one particular day when you knew things had to change, and if so what were the circumstances?

No, I remained blind until long after my cancer and loss of my business.

I know I need to make the changes that are suggested in this book, but if I take time off for myself, my family will suffer tremendous financial loss; how will I handle the guilt?

This answer rests largely in the nourishment found in spiritual truths and understanding. The "mindset" and "guilt" about life, what is important, what brings ultimate happiness…it all revolves around the ego. The soul and the peace to be found rest in accepting as true certain universal principles. I believe firmly that time has no meaning and that life continues after death. I have pieced the puzzle together for myself by way of having lost all that I held so tightly (money, success, professional standing) when I realized that I was much happier as a person and as a soul with all of it gone. However, it is also true I was ready to allow this understanding to penetrate (for me). I write about how I arrived at such this place of peace in both of my books, "A Soft Landing" and "Today Creates Tomorrow". I found my peace deep within my own heart.

Is it really possible to live completely stress free? What about so-called "good" stress, don't we need to retain some of that in our lives?

Yes – good stress has a purpose. It is there to help in creativity, it aids in motivation and it provides and it is energizing. Good stress feels good. The process of destruction begins when several other factors come into play. Recognizing the warning symptoms described within this book is the place to start.

What is the biggest challenge in trying to become a "former stressaholic," and what will I need to do to avoid a relapse?

Actually, once you accept and fully understand the destructive nature of having been a stressaholic and you've had a chance to taste what life is like without all that stress, you can develop (as I did) an inner shield, an immunity, that does not allow "stress" in any form to take hold. I do not allow stress to linger. I stop and stomp on anything which could once again ignite for me the condition I suffered with for so long. It is an immediate reflex which lives inside me now and forever.

Recommended Reading

1. The American Institute of Stress – www.stress.org
   The American Institute of Stress has an excellent website to search current research statistics, information on stress management techniques, lectures and for assistance in getting help.

2. Stressaholic – Heidi Hanna, Ph.D.

3. Stress Management for Dummies – Allen Elkin

4. Kill Stress Before it Kills you – Mathew J. Culligan and Keith Sedlacek, MD

5. My Name is John and I am a Stressaholic – John Manager (kindle)

Books by Stacey Blake

A Soft Landing
How One Woman Survived a Collision Course with Death

Today Creates Tomorrow
How Destiny Lies in Your Own Hands

If you wish to contact the author you may visit her website at http://staceyblake.com

www.ingramcontent.com/pod-product-compliance
Ingram Content Group UK Ltd.
Pitfield, Milton Keynes, MK11 3LW, UK
UKHW041822200726
13854UKWH00001BA/442